The Word Whiz's Guide to California Elementary School Vocabulary

By Chris Kensler

A Paper Airplane Project

New York • Toronto

Kaplan Publishing
Published by Simon & Schuster, Inc.
1230 Avenue of the Americas
New York, NY 10020

For bulk sales to schools, colleges, and universities, please contact: Order Department, Simon & Schuster, 100 Front Street, Riverside, NJ 08075. Phone: 1-800-223-2336. Fax: 1-800-943-9831.

Kaplan® is a registered trademark of Kaplan, Inc.

Cover Design: Cheung Tai
Interior Page Design and Production: Paper Airplane Projects

Manufactured in the United States of America

September 2001

10 9 8 7 6 5 4 3 2 1

Library of Congress Cataloging-in-Publication Data

ISBN 0-7432-1098-0

All of the practice questions in this book were created by the authors to illustrate question types. They are not actual test questions.

Table of Contents

About the Author

Chris Kensler grew up in Indiana and attended Indiana University, where he majored in English. He has edited several test prep publications, worked as feature writer/reporter for a daytime drama publication, and written a book or two, including *Study Smart Junior*, which received the Parents' Choice Award. Currently, he is the editor of an art magazine, is married to the lovely woman who designed this book, and has some cool cats and a dog named Joe.

Les Angeles is a figment of his imagination.

Acknowledgments

The author would like to thank Maureen McMahon, Lori DeGeorge, and Beth Grupper for their help in shaping and editing the manuscript, and Chris Dreyer for copyediting this book.

The publisher wishes to thank
Melanie Meredith for her contributions to this book.

Introduction

Hi. My name is Les. Les Angeles. Please, keep your jokes to yourself. I have heard them all.

I am in the fifth grade. I live in, you guessed it, Los Angeles, California. I am a surfing fanatic, a pretty good soccer player, and a vocabulary whiz kid. You name the word, I know its definition. Especially the words they use on the STAR Program (Standardized Testing and Reporting) test. As a matter of fact, any word you are supposed to know by the fifth grade—I know it. But I'm not here to brag. I'm here to help.

I am here for parents, guardians, siblings, and teachers of elementary-school kids in the great state of California—for everyone who wants to help students learn the vocabulary words they need to know. Let me be your guide to Word Whiz-ardry.

And if I can't turn your student into a word whiz like me, I can at least teach her a few more important vocabulary words—words that will help her in school, on the STAR Program test, and in life.

Why Students Blank on Tests

Some kids mess up on tests because they don't understand the question, not because they don't know the answer. My good friend Larry reads all the time, but when a test poses the question "What is the best summary of this story?" he gets nervous, because all the answers look pretty good. My other friend Judith is a math whiz, but just last week she got stumped on a math problem that asked her which number is "greatest." She thought it meant which number was really, really cool, not which number was the "biggest."

This is where *Word Whiz* comes in. This book builds a bridge from the words your student does know to the ones they use on the STAR Program test and other tests. Learning vocabulary this way makes it easier to remember and harder to forget.

Building a bridge is an active thing, so these are active exercises. They do not involve straight memorization—that's been proven to be a bad way for your student to remember words for anything longer than a day. *Word Whiz* exercises involve doing fun things like watching TV, reading magazines, drawing, and using one's imagination.

Lots of the exercises are also designed to become a part of your student's

WhizTip
Hey you—the adult who bought this book—way to go! Education is a team game. Just like a surfer needs a good board, your student needs you to help her stay on top of the learning waves. Or something like that.

everyday life—as much a part as soccer or band practice. That way, the words can seep deep into the brain, so not only are you preparing your student for the STAR Program test, but for all the big tests to come.

How to Use This Book

The book is divided into two parts—the exercises and my Word Whiz word list. The exercises cover words in five major categories: test instructions, English-language arts, math, history-social science, and science. Off to the side of the exercises you'll see a series of icons. These tell you what "materials" the exercises employ—TV, magazines, the Internet, etc. Here they are:

Life   **School**   **Movie**   **Sports**   **Magazine**

History   **Imagination**   **News**   **Internet**   **Television**

On each exercise page, I also provide a **WhizTip,** a **WhizWord,** or an **On the Test** tip. A **WhizTip** gives more information on how you can help your student. A **WhizWord** is an extra vocabulary word related to the ones covered in the exercise. An **On the Test** tip shows you specifically how the vocabulary word has been used on past STAR Program tests.

Lots of the exercises involve writing a story or a sample sentence. Not only will this help with learning the words, it will also help your student improve her writing skills. For this book, and for all schoolwork your student should:

- Write legibly
- Use complete sentences with appropriate punctuation and capitalization
- Spell the words correctly
- Identify and properly use past, present, and future verb tenses

The WhizWord word list at the back of this book has "everyday" definitions for the most important words. If your student hasn't heard of some of these words yet, don't panic! It's possible she hasn't made it to that stage in her curriculum yet. If you are working with a second or third grader, just make sure you discuss the words she doesn't know. That way she'll be getting a little jump-start for when they start using these words on a regular basis in class.

But enough of my yakkin'—let's boogie.

All-Purpose
WhizCards: Part I

In this age of computers, the Internet, and the Sony PlayStation, it's hard to believe that one of the best ways to review words is still the old 3 x 5 flashcard. I keep waiting for Nintendo to come out with something on the Gameboy to replace flashcards, but it hasn't happened yet.

Flashcards work for a few reasons. Reason 1: By writing down the word and its definition on the card, your student's brain has a better chance of storing it than it does simply by reading the word. Reason 2: Flashcards are a good way to whittle down a group of words to the ones your student is really having trouble with. If she starts out with 100 flashcards and after a couple run-throughs is only having trouble with 30 of them, you both know which words to focus on. Reason 3: They are extremely portable. Your student can take them anywhere anytime. A few minutes of review on the way to church, dinner out, or an international surfing competition quickly start to add up.

WhizTip

It is extremely important for you to praise your student for his progress, and if possible, set up an awards system for this exercise. (My dad gives me surfing decals.) Make it something he looks forward to, not a chore.

MAKING WHIZCARDS EXERCISE

Get a pack of colorful index cards. Choose one color and one of the five categories of vocabulary words in this book (Test Instructions, English Language Arts, Math, History-Social Studies, Science). It can be a subject you are both interested in or a subject in which your student needs to build her confidence.

Have your student print the WhizWord in large, legible letters on one side of an index card. Talk about the word. Have your student use it in a sentence. Try to think of clues or tricks she can use to remember it. Now you (the adult) write the definition and any clues or sentences your student came up with on the reverse side. (Use your best handwriting like they taught you in school all those years ago!)

Try to make 20-25 WhizCards a day, completing one subject before moving on to the next, until you have a complete set of WhizCards. (You can do more if your student is enjoying herself, fewer if she is getting stressed.)

By making these WhizCards, you will automatically improve your student's familiarity and comfort with a lot of new words. You will also know which words (and subjects) she needs the most work on. And, most importantly, you will be able to play all of the cool games on the next page.

All-Purpose
WhizCards: Part II

WhizTip
Remember, your student has enough worries in his life—probably more than you did at his age. Try to keep your vocabulary work with him as enjoyable as humanly possible.

Ever since my parents got the deluxe cable package, I've been watching the Game Show Network. It has reruns of classic game shows from the '60s, '70s and '80s. The clothes worn by the game show hosts and contestants are ... incredible. Where did anyone ever get the idea that big pointy collars and lots of chest hair is attractive? Anyway, all of the classic game shows have given me a couple of classic ideas for games you and your student can play using WhizCards.

WHIZCARD GAMES

Guess Again!

You need 2-4 players (two on each team) and a stopwatch or egg timer to play. One person on each team picks five WhizCards. That player tries to get the other person on the team to guess what the word on the WhizCard is by giving clues, without saying the word. The clue-giver can—and should!—say the definition, and think up other hints.

Each team has one minute to try to get through all five WhizCards. For example, after the first round, the score could be "three words correct" to "two words correct" (3-2). Each team then picks five more words and the team members switch places (the one who was guessing is now giving the clues). You keep playing like this until one team gets 20 words correct.

But you can also play Guess Again! with just two people. If you do, see how long (how many minutes) it takes to get 20 words correct. Play the game regularly and try to beat your own best record. (Note: It's important to discuss the words your team couldn't figure out after each round.)

Whiz Draw

To play, you need 2-10 players, a stopwatch or egg timer, and a big pad of paper. (Whiz Draw is best played with one of those big poster-sized pads of paper, but a regular-size notebook works, too.) Divide the players into two teams. One player on each team picks out five WhizCards. That "artist" has two minutes to draw pictures that describe each word. The artist cannot speak or write any words! Keep playing, alternating between the teams, until one team gets 20 words correct.

Whiz Draw is the most fun when you play with lots of friends and family members, but you can play it with just two people. If you do, see how long it takes to get 20 words correct, with you and your student switching every five words from "artist" to "word-guesser." Play the game regularly and try to beat your own best record, and discuss the words your student couldn't figure out.

Test Instructions
Place Relationships

My locker at school is just how I like it. While teachers have called it "a stinking mess" and "scary bordering on dangerous," I disagree. To me, it is a work of art. And I know where everything is.

My math book and my gym socks are on **top** of my social studies book. My homework and my notebooks are crammed between my trumpet case and my collection of decaying apples. (Mom always packs me an apple for lunch—I hate apples.) The **inside** of my locker is a perfect mirror of my personality—a misunderstood, sloppy genius. The **outside** is plastered with stickers of my favorite bands—Limp Bizkit and Kid Rock—and teams—the Raiders and the Dodgers.

Why am I telling you all this? Because tests often use words that describe where things are. Your student should become as comfortable with them when he is taking a test as when he is describing his locker. These are also the kind of words that you just assume a student understands. And he probably does. But you have to make sure, because they are used very often on the tests taken by students in California.

WhizTip

Remember! When you are asking your student these test-type questions, write them down whenever you can. Your student needs to see the words on paper, not just hear them, so she recognizes them on the test.

LOCKER OR CLOSET EXERCISE

Use your student's closet, bedroom, locker, or book bag as the subject for your questions. Get paper and pencil and write one question for each of the "Place Relationship" words. For example:

Which of the following is at the <u>bottom</u> of your bookbag?
A. a can of Spam
B. extra-credit science project
C. a two-month old baloney sandwich
D. a Nerf football

On <u>top</u> of which piece of your clothing did I find moldy pizza last week?
A. your sweat socks
B. your pajamas
C. your new white shirt
D. your solar-powered-fan safari hat

Answers: A, C (Boy was Dad mad!)

Do this exercise three separate times—I suggest once a week for three weeks—to reinforce this important vocabulary.

Test Instructions

Facts and Opinions

On the Test

Which of the following are correct and which are incorrect?

When your student is reading about stuff she likes, it's pretty easy to remember what she just read. For example, I'm a surfing fan. I just read the biography of surfing legend Corky Carroll, about how he started surfing professionally as a teenager, has never had a real job, and basically made the sport what it is today. If you ask me a question about that book and give me four answer choices, I'm probably going to get it the answer right.

What's the correct way to write this sentence?

But let's say you ask me questions about something I find really boring and stupid—like Britney Spears. It is harder to figure out the **facts** and **opinions** in a story you have no interest in. How am I supposed to remember what her favorite song is on her new album? I could care less!

READING STUFF THEY LIKE EXERCISE

You are going to use reading materials that your student actually likes to get her used to separating facts from opinions, and to get her used to seeing the words correct and true.

Pick out a piece of writing that has both facts and opinions. I suggest movie, music, book, and television reviews.

Your student is going to:
1) Answer two questions about the review (that you will write).
2) Pick out one fact from the review.
3) Pick out one opinion from the review.

So first, you need to write down a fact/opinion question and a correct/true question. Here is an example of each:

Which of the following is the opinion of the writer?
A. *Digimon* is a good show.
B. *Digimon* is a bad show.
C. *Digimon* is going off the air.
D. *Digimon* is on too early.

From the review, which statement is true?
A. *Digimon* is really popular.
B. *Digimon* is not popular at all.
C. *Digimon* is a show about snails.
D. *Digimon* is going to be made into a movie.

Have your student read the review and tackle your fact/opinion questions. Then ask your student to identify one additional fact and opinion in the review. Do this with three reviews, or until you are confident your student is comfortable with the "Facts and Opinions" words.

Test Instructions
Mostly and Mainly

One of the keys to doing well on the STAR Program test and other standardized tests is the ability to grasp the **main idea** in a reading passage. In most reading passages, there are a lot of words, but there is usually one **main idea**—what the passage is **mostly** about.

The **main idea** is the concept that the writer is most concerned with getting across. In magazines and newspapers, the **main idea** of an article is usually summed up in the article's headline or title.

A good way to train your student's brain to figure out what reading passages are **mainly** about is to practice with commercials on TV and in the advertisements in magazines and newspapers. After all, the whole point of advertising is to get across a **main idea** as quickly and powerfully as possible.

Like: If you don't use our deodorant, you will stink and no one will like you. Or: If you don't use our website, your business will go bankrupt and you will be very, very unhappy.

On the Test

What is the main idea of the story you just read?

What is the story mostly about?

If Suzanne reaches into her pocket and selects one dime, which year will most likely be on the dime?

COMMERCIALS AND ADVERTISING EXERCISE

Let's start with magazine ads. First, get a piece of paper and a pencil. Now grab a copy of something your student reads on his own. Pick out three ads and write one question for each ad, using the "Mostly and Mainly" phrases and words. For example, there is an ad for a cool new backpack with the slogan "It's all about style." So you could write:

According to this ad, what is their backpack mainly about?
A. If you carry this backpack, you will be happy.
B. If you carry this backpack, you will be stylish.
C. If you carry this backpack, your books will be safe.
D. If you carry this backpack, you will be laughed at.

Answer: B

Use advertisements for things your student likes—it will make it easier to keep his attention and make the exercise fun. Here are a few suggestions on where to look: your student's favorite magazines, your student's favorite television shows, and the movie trailers at the beginning of movies that you rent. Keep repeating this exercise until you've used each of the "Mostly and Mainly" phrases three times.

Words Covered
abbreviation, adjective, adverb,
antonym, conjunction, modifier,
noun, preposition, pronoun,
proper noun, synonym,

English-Language Arts
Parts of Speech

Come close. A little closer. I have something important to tell you. Not only should your student learn what all these vocabulary words mean, she should also learn what parts of speech the words are.

No big deal—there are only a few parts of speech. Its not like we're ancient Egyptians dealing with hieroglyphs—where every picture is representing a totally different thing.

PARTS OF SPEECH EXERCISE

Have your student photocopy a page out of her favorite book or magazine. It can be *Harry Potter*, *Ranger Rick*—whatever. Now pick three sentences and have your student copy them onto lined paper, with a blank line separating each line of the sentence. Have her label every word on that page with a part of speech.

To make sure your student sticks with it, do this exercise with him, armed with this book (all the parts of speech in the list above are explained in the Whizword list in the back of this book) and your trusty *Elements of Style*, if you need it. When she comes to a word she doesn't know, discuss it and figure out what kind of word it must be. Here's an example from a story from the NASCAR website:

prep.	pro.	adj.	noun	prep.	art.	adj.
In	his	first	start	for	the	potent

adj.	noun	proper noun
Holman-Moody Ford	team,	Fireball Roberts

v.	art.	adv.	adj.	n.	con.	v.
leads	the	final	eight	laps	and	wins

art.	proper noun
the	Southeastern 500.

Repeat this exercise with three different pieces of reading material. Different kinds of writing use different kinds of words. Newspapers use a bunch of verbs and proper nouns. Fiction uses a bunch of adjectives and adverbs.

Important: Don't do all three sample passages in a row—you don't want your student to get sick of grammar. Do them over the course of a few days or a week. That way she will have time to learn the parts of speech at a pace that lets her brain absorb them. Spreading things out will also keep her from running away screaming!

English-Language Arts
Writing Tools

I love to read. I just do. I also like to write my own stories. I won a young writers fiction award last year for a story I wrote about a cricket and his adventures in California wine country. I titled it "Chirpie and Vinnie." Chirpie the Cricket is the **narrator**. He has to find his cousin, Vinnie, because their grandfather passed on (bass bait!) and left them in his will a map to the best vineyards in Sonoma County. That's the **plot**. Vinnie becomes the story's **hero** when he rescues Chirpie from the clutches of evil Carl the Bluejay. They both live happily ever after, munching on the leaves of Farmer Ted's grape leaves.

Anyway, to write my story I used a bunch of the writing tools all writers use. It's important for your student to know what those tools are. Things like **narrator**, **plot**, **hero**, **dialogue**, **imagery**—they're all parts of what make stories fun to read.

WhizTip

If your student is unfamiliar with more than three to four of these words, do the story writing exercise several times, using three to four words each time.

STORY-WRITING EXERCISE

Go over the "Writing Tools" words with your student to gauge his familiarity with them. Mark the ones he has trouble with. Use the WhizWord list in the back of this book to introduce your student to any words that are new to him. Write those words and their definitions down on a piece of paper.

Now set your student up with a pencil and paper or a new Word document on his computer. Give him 30 minutes to write a piece of fiction about his favorite subject. It can be about a superhero who does laundry, a pet cat who does good deeds for strangers, a cricket who visits wine country—anything. Supply your student with the list of words he had trouble with. Have him write his story, focusing on using the words he didn't know.

The words should not be part of the story, but he should use them to tell his story. For example, if he had trouble with imagery and metaphor, he needs to use A LOT of imagery and A TON of metaphors in his story. The story doesn't need to win any awards, it just needs to show he knows what the words mean.

Note: You can also point out examples of these concepts when you are watching TV, in magazines that your student reads, and in movies. (If you point them out during the movies, keep your voice down.)

On the Test
Which words does Bobby use to describe the setting in his essay?

English-Language Arts
Writing a Letter

I wrote a fan letter to my idol, surfing legend Corky Carroll. Corky was the first person ever to make money surfing. Not only that, after 11 years of professional surfing, he retired at age 24. Since then he's done everything from recording albums to selling cars to starring in TV commercials to waiting tables. He is the original beach bum.

Anyway, here's my letter:

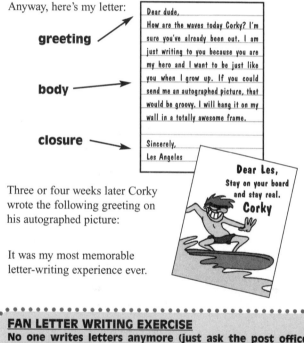

greeting

body

closure

Dear dude,

How are the waves today Corky? I'm sure you've already been out. I am just writing to you because you are my hero and I want to be just like you when I grow up. If you could send me an autographed picture, that would be groovy. I will hang it on my wall in a totally awesome frame.

Sincerely,
Les Angeles

Dear Les,
Stay on your board
and stay real.
Corky

Three or four weeks later Corky wrote the following greeting on his autographed picture:

It was my most memorable letter-writing experience ever.

FAN LETTER WRITING EXERCISE

No one writes letters anymore (just ask the post office). Today, everyone writes e-mails. For this exercise, your student is going to turn back the calendar to 1992, before anyone except some nerds in a computer lab had even heard of e-mail.

Have her write a fan letter to her favorite celebrity. Make sure it includes all of the parts of a letter:

- salutation/greeting
- body
- closure

Have her address it and send it off. (<u>Note</u>: Most celebrity addresses can be found on their official websites.)

English-Language Arts
Parts of a Book

My favorite book right now is Al Davis's biography, *The Silver and Black Life*. My mom got it for me from a used bookstore for my birthday. Even though it's a little bit over my reading level, I've already read it. Twice. It's really cool. It made me think: What would I call my autobiography? And what would it be about?

PUBLISH YOUR AUTOBIOGRAPHY EXERCISE

For this exercise you and your student are going to be physically creating a book. This one will take a week or two, so work on it here and there for a half-hour or an hour at a time. You are going to need a few arts and crafts materials, including a pencil and paper, a stapler, colored markers, and a piece of construction paper.

Now have your student prepare to assemble his book. In pencil, have him write the following words on the top of separate pieces of paper:

Cover
Table of Contents
Chapter 1
Chapter 2
...
Chapter 10
Glossary
Index

Create one chapter for each year of your student's life. Work with your student to think of one important event that happened each year, and use it as a basis for a chapter title. So, for example, after sitting down with my dad, I figured out the following title for my book's fourth chapter:

Chapter Four: She Broke My Teeth, But Not My Spirit

It's about when my big sister "accidentally" knocked my two front teeth out while we were rollerblading. After you have titled the chapters, create your Table of Contents, listing the chapters. Have your student write each chapter. You can help by reviewing family photo albums with your student to jog his memory. It's important to have enough words in each chapter for the Glossary and Index.

Next, show your student an Index and Glossary in a book and discuss their functions. Have him circle the words for his own Index in his book, and underline the words he'll define in the Glossary. Help him organize the words alphabetically, then move to the cover. Think of a fun title and write it on the construction paper with the author's name. Have your student decorate the cover, then go get him a treat—he has earned it!

WhizWord

draft—n.
Most writers
have to go
through a series
of drafts before
their book is
ready to be
published.

English-Language Arts
Answer Words

Leave it to tests to make reading scary. Not only do us kids have to read things we wouldn't otherwise touch with a ten-foot pole, but we also have to explain what we just read! Tests ask us to answer questions like "**support** your theory" or "**summarize** the story" or "**paraphrase** the writer's opinion of green eggs and ham." It's enough to make a young reader long for the days of *See Spot Run*.

But those simple times are gone forever. So it is important for you to make sure your student knows what these "Answer Words" mean. All of these words urge the reader to become actively involved with what she just read, which is kind of what this book does. The best way to get her used to doing this on tests is to get her used to doing it with reading material she actually likes.

FAVORITE BOOKS AND MAGAZINES EXERCISE

Ask your student to pick out two different pieces of reading material. It can be the latest *TV Guide*, her brother's *Car & Driver*, Leo Tolstoy's *War and Peace*—whatever. Now you choose one short reading passage from each. Keep it short—no longer than one page.

Read each passage yourself and write down three questions. For example, for a *Soap Opera Digest* story about a hot young actor, you could write "Summarize why Ben Starrington thinks he will be the next Tom Cruise" and "Paraphrase Ben Starrington's acting philosophy" and "Support the theory that Ben Starrington is an idiot."

Have your student write a response to each question. Check her responses. In all cases, it is important for your student to base her response on details from the reading passage. Her answers should identify the sections in the reading passage that support her conclusions. For example:

Support the theory that Ben Starrington is an idiot.
Ben Starrington is obviously an idiot because he thinks Leo Tolstoy is the actor who played the cowardly lion in the *Wizard of Oz*, he thinks Christina Aguilera has a better voice than Barbra Streisand, and his favorite food is wheat germ.

On the Test
Which one is the best summary of the story?

English-Language Arts
Kinds of Writing

There are all different kinds of writing, but they can be roughly grouped into four categories: true stories, make-believe stories, **drama**, and **poems**.

By true stories— also called **nonfiction**—I mean stories based on facts. For example, **biographies** and **autobiographies** are based on real lives. (I just finished reading a biography of the pilot Amelia Earhart. It was great.)

Make-believe stories—also called **fiction**—include **fantasy** and **fables**. (The *Harry Potter* series is a perfect example of **fantasy fiction**.) **Dramas** are stories written for the stage and screen. Any TV show, movie, or play you see is a **drama**. And then there is **poetry**. One thing to remember about **poetry** is it usually rhymes, but not always! (I know, not much of a rule, but it's the best I can do.)

When your student is tackling a reading comprehension passage on the STAR Program test or another test, he needs to note what kind of writing it is. That will help him answer the questions about it.

WhizTip

The more time you spend in libraries and bookstores with your student, the more comfortable he will feel with books, reading, and using new words.

TREASURE HUNT EXERCISE

For this exercise, you are going to need books. Lots of them. So get in a plane, train, or automobile and get yourself and your student over to the library or your local bookstore.

You are going to be sending your student on a series of treasure hunts while you sit back and sip a cafe latte or thumb through a newspaper. Send him out into the library or bookstore or your house to find one example of each of the "Kinds of Writing" words. For example, send him out to find a book of poems and a book of plays. Depending on how well your student knows these words, you can explain what each one means before your student goes on his search. When he brings the books back, ask him why he chose each one.

Keep sending him out on these scavenger hunts until he has located each of the kinds of writing. (Note: He can also ask bookstore salespeople or a librarian for help along the way—just make sure your student is the one doing the talking, not you.) As a reward, check out or purchase the book he likes best. My mom did this with me—that's how I got my Corky Carroll biography!

Math
Kinds of Numbers

My mom and dad have always been obsessed with gasoline prices. And with the recent turmoil surrounding high energy costs in California, their obsession has gotten even worse. My dad will drive for miles and miles to save 2 cents a gallon. I try to point out that perhaps driving all those extra miles and using all of that extra gas might counteract how much he is saving, but it doesn't seem to make an impression.

My mom has gotten into the habit of going to a website that has the current gas prices at local gas stations before she goes out to fuel up. This plan seems more rational to me. Unfortunately, she drives a big SUV that guzzles gas, so she is on that website a lot. Unless gas prices drop really fast, or my parents sell their big cars for subcompacts, trying to minimize the cost of gas is going to be a big family project for the foreseeable future.

On the Test

What is the smallest whole number you can make using the digits 2, 3, 8 and 3?

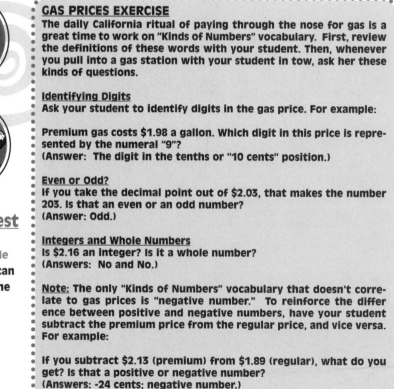

GAS PRICES EXERCISE
The daily California ritual of paying through the nose for gas is a great time to work on "Kinds of Numbers" vocabulary. First, review the definitions of these words with your student. Then, whenever you pull into a gas station with your student in tow, ask her these kinds of questions.

Identifying Digits
Ask your student to identify digits in the gas price. For example:

Premium gas costs $1.98 a gallon. Which digit in this price is represented by the numeral "9"?
(Answer: The digit in the tenths or "10 cents" position.)

Even or Odd?
If you take the decimal point out of $2.03, that makes the number 203. Is that an even or an odd number?
(Answer: Odd.)

Integers and Whole Numbers
Is $2.16 an integer? Is it a whole number?
(Answers: No and No.)

Note: The only "Kinds of Numbers" vocabulary that doesn't correlate to gas prices is "negative number." To reinforce the difference between positive and negative numbers, have your student subtract the premium price from the regular price, and vice versa. For example:

If you subtract $2.13 (premium) from $1.89 (regular), what do you get? Is that a positive or negative number?
(Answers: -24 cents; negative number.)

Math
Symbols and Variables

It's important for your student to get comfortable with the different kinds of numbers. He should add them, subtract them, multiply them, divide them, group them, list them in order, etc. Once your student can do these things, he can progress to the next exciting stage in math—conceptual thinking!

Instead of using numbers that "are there" to get an answer, your student needs to realize that **symbols** can take the place of numbers, and have meanings all their own. So it is important for him to understand what the words surrounding **variables** mean.

WhizWords
When you solve for an unknown, you usually wind up with one or more of the following:

quotient
remainder
result

THE GREAT UNKNOWN EXERCISE
Luckily, variables and symbols aren't confined to math problems. They appear in "real life" all of the time. So, of course, that's where we will go to improve the understanding of these words!

Symbols
Symbols are everywhere. They are basically shorthand for words and phrases, kind of like the hieroglyphs used by the ancient Egyptians. Work with your student to come up with ten common symbols you see in everyday life. They can be logos for TV networks or sports teams, symbols used to denote money, letters that stand for a trademark—anything that uses a symbol to stand for something else.

Represents
Once you have collected a group of symbols, have your student re-draw the symbol and write a sentence explaining what each one represents. Make sure she uses the word "represents" in her sentence. For example:

The symbol $ represents "money" or "dollars."
The symbol ™ represents "trademark." That means someone owns that name.

Variables
Have your student pick three easy-to-draw symbols. Now *you* write three math problems for each symbol (that makes nine total), using the symbols as variables in the problem. For example:

$3 + ™ + 4 = 10$
What does the variable ™ represent in this problem?

Do this one symbol at a time. By working with symbols your student already knows he will learn that symbols (like ™ and $, like *x* and *y*) can mean anything you want them to mean in a math problem. They are variables.

On the Test
Find for each pair of fractions the sum, difference, product, and quotient.

19

Math
Word Problems

WhizWord

round—v.
to go to the nearest number. After combining the two values, round to the nearest whole number.

Sometimes students struggle with math problems not because the problems are hard, but because they are worded in a confusing way. Your student may be a whiz when it comes to **addition**, **subtraction**, **multiplication**, and **division**, but she may freeze when faced with a question like, "Amy has twice as many of which coins as she has quarters?" Many math problems are presented as word problems, so your child has to figure out what type of math operation is needed to solve the word problem.

Ironically, vocabulary is often the key to solving math problems. You can help your child become a whiz on math tests by getting her used to recognizing the "hidden clues" in word problems. This activity will help your child recognize "How much money did he spend altogether?" as a signal for **addition** and "How many shirts were removed from the clothesline?" as a signal for **subtraction**.

MATH TEST SYNONYMS EXERCISE

For this exercise, you are going to have your student create a list of words that could be used in math problems to represent addition, subtraction, multiplication, and division. For example, "combine" is a word that can be used in place of "add." Work with your student to find at least three synonyms for each. My dad and I worked on "addition" synonyms and came up with the following:

Addition Words
combine
join
mix

Here is a jump start for creating lists for the remaining words:

Subtraction Words	Multiplication Words	Division Words
remove	triple	share

Once you have come up with a list of three synonyms for each these words, write a sample test question for each. For example:

If Maude removes three nose hairs, how many nose hairs will she have left?

They can be as nonsensical (above) or realistic as your student wants. The point is to get her used to seeing these words, and using them herself.

Note: If you are having trouble coming up with synonyms, use a thesaurus and choose three of the words that you think would be most likely to appear in a grade school word problem.

Math
Number Relationships

There are four math words that mean similar things and are easy to get confused: **mean, median, mode,** and **average**. Let's just quickly review.

- **Mean** and **average** are the same thing—it is what you get by adding some numbers together, then dividing by how many numbers you added up.
- **Median** is the middle one in a group of numbers. The same amount of numbers are above it and below it.
- The **mode** is the one that occurs the most number of times.

To remember these words, we are going to use a couple techniques. First, let's use some word association.

- **Mean** "means" **average**, and **average** "means" **mean**. That's the way you remember those two are the same thing.
- **Median** is the middle number. Think of a **median** that divides a highway or boulevard. It runs right down the middle of the road. So does the **median** in a set of numbers—it is the number in the middle.
- **Mode** sounds like the word "most." The **mode** is the number that occurs most often in a set.

WhizTip

Did you know you can find additional information on California standards online? **(Try to control your excitement.)** Just go to the NCITE site at: http://ncite.lausd.k1 2.ca.us/index.html. The site has separate sections for adults, teachers, and students.

USING RECENT TEST SCORES EXERCISE

Now that your student has an easy way to remember which word is which, he can practice recognizing them.

Have him gather up all of his tests for a particular class. It can be for any class, but why not use math class as long as you're at it. Sort them from lowest to highest scores and find the values above. For example, I just gathered my math tests and quizzes we have taken so far. Here are my scores from lowest to highest:

34, 71, 83, 83, 92, 99, 99, 99, 110 (I got extra credit on that one)

Mean and Average	= 34+71+83+83+92+99+99+99+110 ÷ 9
	= 85.56
Median	= 92 (this test score is the middle value)
Mode	= 99 (this test score occurs three times)

Do this for the tests from three different classes. If your student's school doesn't give percentages, or you would rather not use test scores, you can also use: a baseball team's batting averages, the points or rebounds for the players on a basketball team, a quarterback's passing attempts and completions for a series of games

Note: If there is an even number of test scores or numbers, the median is the average of the two numbers in the middle.

Math

Fractions and Decimals

What makes somebody "cool" depends on who is defining "cool." A bunch of soccer players might think the best soccer player is the coolest. A bunch of kids in an Internet chat room might think the one with the best home page is the coolest. A bunch of kids who follow surfing would definitely think the one who got an autographed picture of Corky Carroll is the coolest. (That's me.) Cool is definitely in the eye of the be-cooler.

What does this have to do with **fractions** and **decimals**? Just be cool, I'm getting to that.

There's nothing truly cool about **fractions** and **decimals**, but coolness can definitely be measured using **fractions**. If your student is having trouble remembering the words that describe **fractions** and **decimals**, tell him to be cool, and try the following.

COOL EXERCISE

Get a pencil and paper. Have your student write down five television shows (or movies or bands or baseball players). Have him list them in order of coolness.

Now, write down a question and ask him to express the show's coolness with a fraction or a decimal. For example:

How much cooler is *Survivor* than *Friends*?
Answer: 1.25 times as cool. (That's just my opinion.)

Now ask two questions about his answer. For example:

1) Where is the decimal point in that number?
2) What is that decimal expressed as a fraction?

Answers: 1) Between the 1 and the 2.
                 2) 1 1/4.

Keep going until you can't think of any more questions. Like: How many cool castaways are there on *Survivor*, compared to uncool castaways? Express that as a ratio.

And so on. Continue this exercise until you have used each of the "Fractions and Decimals" words three times. (This may take a couple separate sessions. Cool?)

Math

Graph Words

There are three kinds of graphs we will all be seeing and using for the rest of our lives. Knowing what they are—and how to read them—is important when taking the STAR Program test and getting around in today's statistics-obsessed world.

To remember which graphs are which is fairly easy.

Line graphs typically look like mountains, some rocky, some rolling.

Bar graphs typically resemble some sort of weird staircase.

Circle graphs (also called pie graphs) look like—pies.

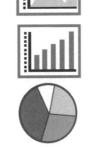

On the Test

Use the data in the table to complete the bar graph for ages 8 and 9.

. . . .

USING GRAPHS EXERCISE

Have your student use the three different kinds of graphs to explain how things important to him can be represented in graph form.

For instance, after your student sees a movie on TV or at the theater, ask him to show how much of the movie was about the characters, the plot, and the setting using a pie chart. Have him do this after every movie so he understands how pie charts are used. You can do the same thing with a situation comedy on TV. Have him divide a show by which characters the show focuses on.

Line graphs are typically used to measure something over time. So have your student trace one of his interests over time. If he has a favorite daily cartoon or comic, have him give it a rating from 1–10 each time he sees it, and have him chart the results with a line graph.

For a bar graph, you could have your student chart the number of tests he has every week over the course of a month.

These are just suggestions. The point is to use events and activities from your student's life to reinforce how information is presented on a graph. Make sure he always labels the graph correctly, and make sure you ask questions based on the graph he has drawn.

Math

Lines

On the Test

Let *CD*, *EF* be
perpendicular
diameters of a
circle, as shown.

The ability to define which way a line "points"—**horizontal**, **vertical**, **diagonal**—or how two lines are related to each other—**parallel**, **perpendicular**—is important on many California elementary school math tests.

When I think of how lines intersect, I think of Bart Simpson riding his skateboard through Springfield as the credits roll on *The Simpsons* TV show. If you drew his route on a map, you would have all kinds of lines.

SKATES AND SKATEBOARDS EXERCISE

Ask your student to think about where she goes on her wheels. Most kids these days have either a skateboard, rollerblades, scooter, or bicycle. (My mom never even learned how to ride a bicycle, but that's another story.)

Have your student draw a simple map of her journey the last time she used her rollerblades, skateboard, or bicycle. If she can't remember the last time—tell her to get some fresh air! Then have her draw the diagram showing where she went. Here is mine from my bike ride yesterday.

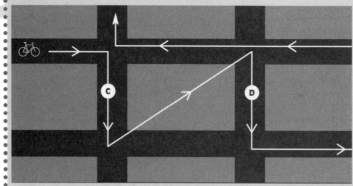

WhizTip

If your student
isn't up to going
on a bike ride,
you can have
her draw a
diagram of
any kind of
activity—like
walking around
a grocery store,
or riding the
bus to school.

Now label some of the lines she drew and write three questions about the map she gives you, using the words above. Here's a sample question my mom wrote about my map:

How are lines C and D related to each other?
A. The are perpendicular.
B. They are parallel.
C. They are vertical.
D. They are diagonal.

Answer: B.

Math

Angles

It is not enough to know what an angle is. Your student needs to be able to indentify many of the different types of angles. The thing is, the words used to describe angles are not everyday words. Terms like **obtuse** and **congruent** are enough to frighten any student.

To get to know all the different types of angles, ask your student to imagine something way different than math class—a game that inspires fear in even the bravest of my fellow students.

Dodge ball.

What kid doesn't worry about the game of dodge ball. If he's not thinking about pegging an arch enemy or a big-talking friend, he's thinking about evading the same people as they try to peg him themselves. And as everyone knows, dodge ball is all a game of angles.

WhizTip

If dodge ball has been outlawed in your school or you find it idiotic, you can use baseball (draw the angles of the baseball pitched and then hit) soccer (the angles formed by a series of passes) or whatever sport your student is most interested in.

DODGE BALL EXERCISE
Get paper and pencil. Have your student diagram scenes from a dodge ball game. It can be a real or an imagined game. It can be the throw of a ball and the direction it bounced off someone's butt. It can be a particular evasion tactic. Just make sure he draws the angles of the actions in question, like so:

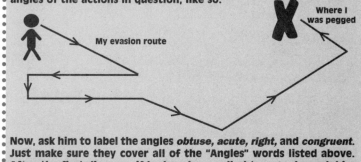

My evasion route

Where I was pegged

Now, ask him to label the angles *obtuse, acute, right,* and *congruent*. Just make sure they cover all of the "Angles" words listed above. After the first diagram, if he has drawn all obtuse angles, ask him to diagram a dodge ball move with acute angles, congruent angles, etc. Make sure he uses and labels each of the angles at least twice.

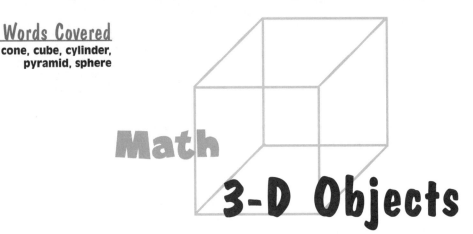

Math
3-D Objects

WhizWords

Words used
when discussing
3-D objects include
plane **and** volume.
So use 'em!

Recognizing different three-dimensional objects is easy enough when you're eating an ice cream cone (3-D object) or watching a TV special about the Egyptian **Pyramids** (3-D objects). But when there is a 3-D object floating on a page on a math test with a scary question next to it, well, real life can fly out the window.

To fight the effects of test-taking tension, a good way to help your student remember basic 3-D objects is to have him draw them himself so he has an active memory of the object.

INVENT A VIDEO GAME EXERCISE

Most kids are into computer games. No matter how much you tell them to get outside, you invariably find them glued to the television, outwitting an evil adversary, hopping their way through an intricate maze, or riding the waves in a simulated Huntington Beach Pro-Am as surfing legend Corky Carroll.

One thing video games do very well, however, is render things in three dimensions. So, for this exercise, your student will create his own video game. It can be whatever he wants, just set some basic guidelines, namely: the video game must include a cone, cube, cylinder, pyramid, and a sphere. Have him write a short description of the game, then have him draw a screen shot involving these five objects. Ask him to label the objects.

Example: 3-Dimensionator

In this game, the sphere-shaped 3-Dimensionator must navigate its way through a 3-D minefield and rescue the Pyramid of Power.

It isn't important how well your student can draw, just that he recognizes what the different objects are, and how they are the same and different from one another. Feel free to have him use this example to work from if he wants.

Words Covered

hexagon, octagon, parallelogram, pentagon, polygon, quadrilateral, rectangle, rhombus, trapezoid, triangle (equilateral and isosceles)

Math

Polygons

A **polygon** is a shape with three or more flat sides. **Polygons** range from the familiar **triangle** to the exotic **rhombus**.

There are a ton of them, and some overlap. For instance, a square is a **rectangle**, but a **rectangle** isn't necessarily a square. A square is also a **rhombus**, but a **rhombus** isn't necessarily a square.

If you think these terms are confusing now, imagine if you were 20 minutes into a math test and you had to answer a question about them!

On the Test

What is the perimeter of this octagon?

CAR SHAPE GAME EXERCISE

No, it's not about the shapes of cars, it's a shape game you can do when you're in the car. But this one could end up costing you.

The next time you and your student are in the car together, take the change out of your pocket or change holder and put it on the dashboard tray or in the cup holder. Start calling out geometric shapes. Tell your student to find a real-world example of the shape. For every one she gets right, she gets a coin.

Start with something easy, like "octagon." All Stop signs are octagons. Go to triangle, rectangle, trapezoid, etc. Tell her to look for the shapes in street signs, architecture, windows, and billboards. You probably won't be able to see them all on a normal drive, but if you play the game often, you will definitely end up a few dollars poorer, and your student will know her polygons much better.

The thing is, even if your student gets one wrong, or she just can't find a parallelogram, she is still thinking and trying to figure out the shapes she sees. For example, you may call out "equilateral triangle!" and she may try to get away with an isosceles triangle—thereby reinforcing isosceles in the process!

Note: Want to spice it up a bit? Do "double or nothing" and have her define the shape after she has correctly spotted it. (Note: This exercise is especially effective when a friend is also in the car providing some healthy competition.)

WhizWord

perimeter—n. Some tests ask for the perimeter of various polygons. The perimeter of a polygon is the length of all its sides added together.

History-Social Science

Exploration

WhizWord

**inhabitants—n.
The people who
live somewhere
already. After
your student has
written his book,
have him write
an epilogue
from the
"discoverees'"
point of view.**

Besides wars, America's history is marked over and over again by **discovery** and **exploration**. From Christopher Columbus sailing from Spain to what he thought was India, to the westward expansion of American settlers, to astronauts poking around in outer space, our culture has always been obsessed with seeing what is on the other side.

So history and social studies tests may include questions about **pioneers** and **explorers**. You don't want your student stumbling over exploration words as she searches for the right answers, do ya? I thought not. Now, most of these words are pretty easy, so I am going to suggest a real fun exercise that will challenge your student's imagination as he learns the vocabulary words.

CLIFFHANGERS EXERCISE

Have your student write a serialized story about discovering a new land. Have him end each story with a cliffhanger—an event that happens right at the end of the chapter that makes you want to turn the page. Use the exploration words in the title of each chapter, in this order.

> **Chapter 1: Explorer**
> **Chapter 2: Navigate**
> **Chapter 3: Discover**
> **Chapter 4: Colonize**
> **Chapter 5: Pioneer**

For example, the first chapter of my story is called "Corky Carroll: Explorer of Secret Beach." The last paragraph has him choosing between entering a dark cave to look for a magic surf board OR relaxing and taking advantage of some prime tanning hours on the beach. (Hint: He chooses the cave.)

Words Covered

commerce,
consumer,
goods,
producer,
profits,
services

History-Social Science
Capitalism and Economics

The United States is a capitalist society. That means individuals own property, they **produce goods** and **services** at their jobs, and they **consume goods** and **services**, too. The companies and individuals who **produce** the **goods** and **services** try to make a **profit**.

Pretty dry stuff for a grade schooler! A good way to reinforce these words is to take an in-depth look at a company that makes a product your student can't get enough of. For instance—I just love Fruity Pebbles cereal. It tastes great and gives me the sugar rush I need to start the day out right.

WhizWord

supply and demand—n. When demand goes up, supply has to go up, too, or things get more expensive.

FAVORITE COMPANY EXERCISE

For this exercise, your student needs to pick out a product she really gets a kick out of. It can be Fruity Pebbles, a magazine, a video game, a bicycle—anything she wants. Once she has chosen a product, you are going to ask her to write five short descriptions using the "Capitalism and Economics" words in relationship to the product. I will use Fruity Pebbles as an example:

● Describe a consumer of Fruity Pebbles
● Describe the producer of Fruity Pebbles
● What types of goods and services would the producers of Fruity Pebbles need to purchase to manufacture and sell their product?
● What kind of employees would you hire if you were an employer at Fruity Pebbles?
● If you owned Fruity Pebbles, what would you do to make the company more profits?

If you want, you can have your student look up the company on the Internet to find some basic information on it—including the number of employees and its profits for the previous year or quarter.

You can also get more specific within each section. For example, for the consumer description, you can have her write down three characteristics that might be common to Fruity Pebbles consumers, such as:

1. A love of Fruity Pebbles
2. Distaste for Sugar Frosted Flakes
3. High sugar tolerance

This is a fun exercise if you work on it together. Take your time and help your student with these new words. When you are done, if you think she could still use more work on them, repeat the exercise, but this time, *you* pick the company, and have your student help *you* write the answers.

History-Social Science
Markets and Trade

WhizWords

export—n., v.
import—n., v.
**I bet your student
has toys and
games, and I bet
they have labels
indicating where
they were made.
On a regular basis,
ask him if a toy is
an** import **(yes/no),
and from what
country it was**
exported.

Words that describe our economy appear often on history and social studies tests. And while your student no doubt knows that CDs, video games, and movies cost money, he may not be sure of the many vocabulary words that go along with everyday transactions.

A good way to have him nail down "Markets and Trade" words is to link them to how he takes part in markets and **trade** himself. For example, for the last year I have been mowing lawns for extra money. It's not glamorous, but it pays great. Anything your student does, or can do, to make money—babysitting, washing cars, selling cookies—will do. What you want him to do for this exercise is to think of his jobs or chores as a business partnership with you. I'll use mowing lawns as my example.

BUSINESS PARTNERS EXERCISE

Get out that pencil and paper. The most important part of a business partnership is figuring out a name. I call my lawnmowing company "Mr. Mow-Man." Write the partnership name at the top of your page.

Now write down the things your student will need to get started. I need:

- lawn mower
- gas
- lawn mowing shoes
- transportation

This is where you get involved. Bargain, barter, and trade with your kid for the stuff he needs to get started. For example, I need to be driven to and from a job once in a while, so I trade one extra night of doing dishes in exchange for a drop off and pick up.

Make a list of the money and/or goods and services you have provided. For the things you have purchased for him, he will be in debt. Put a figure on that debt, either in dollars or in services (washing dishes). Once the business starts, he will have income and services that he can credit against that debt.

After you have shaken hands on the partnership, have him write a short business plan, using all the "Markets and Trade" words, just like any business partner would do.

Note: After he makes some money, take 20 percent of your student's income. Tell him that's the tax he has to pay for living under your roof. (Then give it back—you're just making a point!)

History-Social Science

Monarchies

Living in a democracy is all well and good. We have all these great rights and freedoms. Everyone is created equal and has a bunch of opportunities to make something of themselves. A kid like me can grow up to become a surfing legend like Corky Carroll. Anything could happen. Everything is possible.

But still, wouldn't it be great to be king? You would rule over an **empire** that stretches around the globe. Your **monarchy** would be feared and respected by other countries. And if some little country doesn't fear and respect you, you just grab it and make it part of your **empire**!

King Angeles. It has a nice ring to it.

WhizWord

republic—n. A government made up of representatives elected by the people—a republic is kind of the opposite of a monarchy,

KING OF CALIFORNIA EXERCISE

For this exercise, your student is going to write a short story about how he would rule the state if he were the King of California, using the "Monarchy" words.

Get a pencil and paper. Have your student write down his or her King name at the top. Title the piece: The Reign of (Whatever). Have your student divide the essay into the following four sections:

The Reign of King Angeles
Part I: The Making of a Monarch
Describe how you took power. Did you inherit the position from your parents? Did you have to fight a war?

Part II: A Description of My Empire
Describe the lands you rule over. Is it just California? Do you have colonies on other continents? Are any adjoining states under your control, too?

Part III: Places I Want to Annex Next
Is Nevada high on your list of states to take over next? New Mexico? Why?

Part IV: Temper Tantrums—Examples of My Tyranny
Every king has a bad day. Describe a particularly bad thing you did as king one day when you woke up on the wrong side of bed. Did you get in a war with Arizona? Did you banish outfielder Gary Sheffield for going 0-4 in a big game against the Marlins?

When your student is done, read through the essay with him and see what kind of king he would be!

Words Covered

citizen, Congress, constitution,
democracy, election,
executive branch, federal,
judicial branch, legislature,
unalienable rights

History-Social Science

Government

As the 2000 presidential **election** proved, our system of government is a complicated one, based on checks and balances. The two guys gunning to be top dog of the **executive branch**, Bush and Gore, had to fight in Florida's **legislature** and **judicial branch**, plus the **judicial branch** of the United States.

Of course, it would be a lot easier if we lived under a monarchy and all we had to remember was "the queen is always right, and what she says goes." But then we wouldn't have all these cool **unalienable rights** to do whatever we want, like watch golf highlights on ESPN 2 at 3 o'clock in the morning. (Please don't tell my parents.)

WhizTip

Have your student check her constitution against the Constitution of the United States. See how her country's elections, checks and balances, and rights and responsibilities compare.

CONSTITUTION EXERCISE

Get a pencil and paper. Have your student name a country after herself. Now have her create her own constitution for a democracy, covering these three important parts of democracy: elections, citizens' rights, and the government structure.

Preamble
Write a short summary of your constitution (you may want to do this last).

Citizens' Rights
Cover a citizen's rights using these words:
- liberty
- unalienable rights

Elections
Cover elections using these words:
- democracy
- election

Government
Cover the government using these words:
- checks and balances
- congress
- executive branch
- judicial branch

Note: This is a hard exercise, so spend time with your student working on it. This exercise works best with both of you working together. To keep the fantasy going, ask her to appoint you as the vice president in her country.

History-Social Science
Immigration and Heritage

As you know, America is a country of immigrants. Only a small number of people can claim a direct link to this land. This makes words about immigration and different **customs** a big part of your student's education, because they are words about our country's history—especially in California.

But that doesn't make the words any easier, especially when they appear on a test. So to take the edge off this tough vocabulary, I thought using famous singers, actors, and sports stars might be a good idea.

FAMOUS IMMIGRANTS EXERCISE

Have your student write a short biography of someone he is interested in who immigrated from another country. Have him structure the story with the following headlines, using the following words under each headline:

Celebrity Name
Home country (majority, minority)
Some customs of home country (heritage, customs, tradition)
Why did the celebrity come to the U.S.? (migration)

For example, one of my favorite baseball players is Orlando Hernandez of the New York Yankees. Here's his story.

Celebrity Name
Orlando Hernandez is a major league baseball pitcher. He has a high leg kick. They call him "El Duque."

Home Country
He is from Cuba. When he was there, he was part of the Cuban majority. In the United States, Cubans are a minority.

Customs in Cuba
Some customs in Cuba are smoking cigars and dancing to Cuban music. Cubans have a traditional music I learned about from a documentary called *The Buena Vista Social Club*. It is part of their heritage.

Why He Came to the U.S.
The reason for his migration was simple. He came to play baseball because they wouldn't let him pitch in Cuba anymore.

WhizWord
persecute—v.
Immigrants and minorities are often persecuted in their new land. Persecute means to treat people very badly, usually because of their race or religion.

WhizTip
Share newspaper and magazine articles about immigration with your student and point out these "Immigration and Heritage" words.

Words Covered
**discrimination,
integration,
prejudice,
segregation,
tolerant**

History-Social Science
Civil Rights

You adults have it easy. You get to stay up as late as you want. You get to drive cars. You get to leave your vegetables on your plate if you want. Sometimes, as a kid, watching you exercise all that freedom can get to be a bit much.

A good way to address these "Civil Rights" words it to focus on the stuff a kid has to put up with in an adult world. We can't go to PG-13 or R-rated movies, we can't drive, we can't vote. We have to do everything you tell us to do! It just isn't fair! Some might call it—age **discrimination**!

LITTLE KID EXERCISE

Sorry—I was getting carried away there. But I had a point. For this exercise, have your student write a speech about being a kid in an adult world using the words above.

Grab a pencil and paper. Now have her list three examples of how she, as a kid, is subject to prejudice, discrimination, and segregation. Then have her list three ways how she would like to be integrated better into adult society, and what she will do once she is emancipated from childhood (i.e., turns 18 or 21).

The key is to use at least three of the words in each of her three examples. So instead of writing "Everybody thinks I'm dumb" as one of her examples of anti-kid prejudice, she must write "One kind of prejudice against us kids is everyone thinks we're stupid." She must use the words in her speech.

This exercise requires more deep thought than most, so work with your student to find the three examples. Help your student be creative, and help her write her speech. In case you or your student are stumped, here is one of my examples.

Thanksgiving Discrimination
by Les Angeles

I am segregated from the adults every Thanksgiving when I have to sit at the kids table. This is discrimination against me because I am young. I am obviously smarter than most of the people at the adults' table. They are probably just jealous or scared of my intelligence. I hope that next year they will integrate the big Thanksgiving table and allow us young people to sit there, too.

History-Social Science
War

Your student will learn a lot about wars in his history and social studies classes. Most of the time is spent on the Revolutionary War and the Mexican War of Independence, with a little Civil War and World Wars I and II thrown in.

So it's not a surprise that "War" words show up all the time on tests. Some kids—like my friend Larry—eat this stuff up. Larry can rattle off the generals in all the big Civil War battles. But students like me, with other interests like sports and girls, can have a harder time of it. So a good way to get the words to stick in our heads is to put them on something we all understand—a poster!

Posters aren't just for rock stars and sports heroes. Historically, many nations have used **propaganda** posters to rally their citizens behind their war efforts. The World War II poster featuring Rosie the Riveter is probably the most famous **propaganda** poster, but posters have been a big part of fighting wars for years and years.

WhizTip
Your student's propaganda poster doesn't have to be about a war. It can be about anything he feels strongly about.

PROPAGANDA POSTER EXERCISE

Have your student create a poster for a conflict—it can be any war—using at least five of the words above. Underline the words. Here's one I did for the 1991 Gulf War.

> # Top Golfers Golf in
> # Gulf
>
> Pro golfers Biff Conway and Fred Butlett <u>volunteer</u> for exhibition match in Iraq. Show <u>patriotism</u> and sponsor their match—pledge as little as $1 a stroke. The money you give helps buy the <u>ammunition</u> our troops need. Help our troops force Saddam Hussein to <u>surrender!</u>

Now, there are a ton of "War" words, so he probably won't be able to fit them all on one poster. Have him do two or three posters or flyers, then pick the one he likes best. Display that one on his bedroom wall or somewhere else in the house where he will see it every day.

History-Social Science

Geography

WhizTip

Use this exercise in conjunction with the "Constitution" exercise to see how people and places interrelate. Have your student describe how his government would likely fare on his new continent.

These days, the world is a global village. That means no matter where you live, people on the other **continents** are your neighbors, too. It's mainly because transportation (planes and ships) and technology (satellites and the Internet) are so advanced, you can get from one **continent** to another faster than it used to take to get from one state to another!

But wouldn't it be nice if the global village got a new neighbor? I mean, two-thirds of the Earth is covered by water—even more if global warming keeps melting the polar ice caps. Along with the problems of overpopulation, this means one thing—we need another **continent**! I think putting one smack dab in the middle of the Pacific Ocean would be great.

CREATING THE EIGHTH CONTINENT EXERCISE

For this exercise, your student will be imagining what the eighth continent will look like. Graph paper is best for this exercise, but any paper will do. First, have your student draw a BIG oval with an equator line across the middle. Mark the directions North, South, East, and West on the map. That's the globe. Second, she draws her continent's outline and names it. Third, have her draw different regions on her continent. Fourth, using the "Geography" words, have her create a legend for the different regions. Here is an example of my continent in the middle of the Pacific Ocean. I have named it "Lestopia."

Lestopia: The Eighth Continent

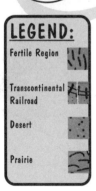

LEGEND:
- Fertile Region
- Transcontinental Railroad
- Desert
- Prairie

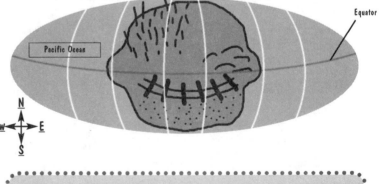

Pacific Ocean

Equator

N W E S

Once your student is done continent building, have her write a short story about how its geography is similar to or different from our continent's geography, using at least three of the "Geography" words. For example: The desert on Lestopia's south coast reminds me of the Painted Desert in Arizona.

History-Social Science
Rebellion

The United States began with an organized rebellion—the Boston Tea Party—and hasn't looked back since. **Revolutions**—both peaceful and violent—have marked our country's history.

Many reading passages on tests use America's rebellious history to measure a student's reading comprehension, so it's important for students to know the words used in relation to the subject. When you are watching, reading, or listening to the news together, make sure you point out **strikes, boycotts,** and revolts going on around the country and the world.

And to further reinforce the vocabulary, make sure you link the words to your student's life.

WhizTip
What revolt or revolution does your student know the most about? The civil rights revolts of the 1960s? The American Revolution? Find out and compare notes.

PROTEST FLYER EXERCISE
Have your student organize a peaceful rebellion against something he thinks is unfair. Washing the dishes, bad cafeteria food, mowing the lawn, taking care of a younger sibling—you name it. In order to gain support for his cause, he needs to create a flyer explaining his position. He must use—and underline—all of the words above in his flyer (this is kind of like the poster exercise we used for the "War" words).

Here is part of a flyer I put together asking my fellow Americans to boycott Jim Carrey movies until my dad lets me see them.

JOIN THE REVOLUTION!
Les Angeles begs you to <u>protest</u> his mean father!
He <u>prohibits</u> Les from watching Jim Carrey movies! For no reason!

Science

Ecosystems

When I think of an **ecosystem**, I think of a damp, misty **wetlands**, full of **diversity**. Lizards are jumping after flying bugs, weird frogs are camouflaged against tree trunks, big green plants and bright flowers are feeding off a ton of **decomposing** plant life. Now that's an **ecosystem**!

But **ecosystems** don't have to be this dramatic. My family has a small backyard behind our house, and there are still a ton of **organisms** interacting back there. We get sparrows that eat the snails that eat the moss (a short **food chain**). Lots of the flowers that my dad plants every year always end up getting eaten by aphids, and his compost pile is packed with rotting greenery and worms. And, of course, our yard is full of weeds that eat the compost when we spread it out on our lawn.

ECOSYSTEMS AROUND YOUR HOME EXERCISE
For this exercise your student is going to describe an ecosystem that occurs near, around—or even in—your house. To start, get a pencil and paper. Have her pick an ecosystem—that's a system where different organisms all interact with each other. It can be a backyard, a nearby field or woods. It can also be as small as a flower box, or even the inside of an apartment (if you have a decent amount of unwanted friends who share the apartment with you!)

Have her list the different organisms in the ecosystem: deer, flowers, possums, pine trees, grass, flies, bacteria, mold, mildew, mosquitoes, bluebirds, roaches, mice, rats, cats, sisters, brothers, etc. When she's done making her list (five to 15 organisms will do) have her write a story about how the organisms interact with each other, using the "Ecosystem" words.

When she's done, have her read it to you and ask her questions about the ecosystem she picked. If some things don't make sense, work on it with her until there is a final version she can keep and reread to brush up on these words. It doesn't have to win the Pulitzer, it just has to include all of the "Ecosystems" words and use them correctly.

Science

Environmentalism

My big sister Aimee is awful when it comes to **recycling**. I am constantly rescuing Mountain Dew cans from the trash can. Probably five or six a day. (She has a serious Mountain Dew problem. She needs help.) For a while I was leaving them in a pile outside her door to make a point. Then she locked me in the attic. So I don't do the can piles anymore.

But it hasn't lessened my resolve to make our house a more **environment**-friendly place. My mom set up separate **recycling** boxes for newspapers, magazines, glass bottles, plastic bottles, and aluminum cans. My dad started a compost pile in the backyard, and last week he said he was thinking about putting a solar panel on the roof! My sister hasn't come around yet, but recently she switched to those three-liter bottles of Mountain Dew, which will reduce the number of cans to be recycled. So I'll count that as progress.

WhizTip

This exercise is an example of how, with a little extra effort, you can use "everyday" activities to reinforce important vocabulary words.

ENVIRONMENT-FRIENDLY HOUSE EXERCISE

How much thought does your family give to conservation? By placing an emphasis on it at home, your student will become familiar with these "Environmentalism" words, and lots of other words that are helpful in class and on tests.

Get a pencil and paper and develop a plan to make your household environment-friendly. There are usually three main areas you can improve:

RECYCLING	**ENERGY**	**POLLUTION**
paper	electricity	car exhaust
	(lights /heat)	(tune-up/new car)
cans		
(aluminum/steel)	fuel (gasoline/oil)	fireplaces
bottles		add plants
(plastic/glass)		(they reduce CO_2)
table scraps		
(compost/leftovers)		

Have your student create a list of ten things your family can do to help protect the environment using the four "Environmentalism" words. Post the list on your refrigerator and encourage your whole family to fulfill the ten environmental goals. After one month, revisit the list and check your family's progress.

Science

Geology

WhizWord

texture—n.
**Different kinds
of rocks have
different** textures.
Igneous rocks
have a lumpy
texture,
sedimentary rocks
are rough, and
metamorphic
rocks **have a
smooth** texture.

Learning about geology is an important part of a grade schooler's science education in California, for obvious reasons! We don't get earthquakes too often in Los Angeles, but huge parts of this state are on shaky ground. So when the Discovery Channel had a show on geology a few weeks ago, I was all eyes.

It turns out that an 18th century gentleman farmer named James Hutton is the guy who figured out the rock cycle. A rock cycle is basically the life cycle of a rock: rocks start out as molten lava that either explodes out of a volcano or stays trapped beneath the Earth's surface. Eventually, it cools and forms **igneous rock** (lava rock). Basalt and granite are common form of **igneous rock**.

That **igneous rock** then goes through a lot of wear and tear. If it gets exposed to the elements on the Earth's surface, it breaks up and turns into stones and gravel and dust. That gets mixed and compacted with other bits and pebbles and forms **sedimentary rock**, like limestone and sandstone.

If that **igneous** and **sedimentary rock** doesn't make it to the Earth's surface, it usually gets reheated and exposed to immense pressure, which squishes it into **metamorphic rock**, like marble.

ROCK WALK EXERCISE

For this exercise you'll need a pencil and paper. Your student is going to create a Rock Walk Tour.

Work with your student to identify the three different rock types in or around your home and neighborhood. Be sure to consider the rocks that your home is actually made of, stones in the yard, or exposed rocks in a nearby park. As you are going along, have your student make a map numbering and identifying the rocks on her rock walk. Here's part of a map that I made.

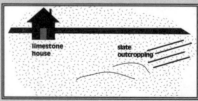

limestone
house

slate
outcropping

Once your student has completed her map, have her give a tour for friends and family. Your student plays the role of the Rock Walk Tour guide, identifying and explaining the different rocks and how they got that way.

Science

Animals

Animals are divided into five categories: **mammals, insects, fish, reptiles,** and **amphibians**. I have had pets representing each of these—hamster, ant farm, tropical fish, a lizard, and a frog. But that's beside the point. The point is, all of these animals interact in nature.

WhizWords

food chain—n.
predator—n.
prey—n.
In a food chain,
the animal that
is a predator is
often also
the prey.

ANIMAL FOOD CHAIN EXERCISE

I am going to give you two food chains. First, have your student do some research on the animals and find out which kind of animals they are. Second, have your student label the animals on the food chain with their classification (reptile, fish, etc.). Third, have him write a short explanation for each, explaining why the animal is a mammal, insect, fish, reptile, or amphibian.

fly   minnow   frog   snake   hawk

_____   _____   _____   _____   _____

smelt   penguin   seal   shark   human

_____   _____   _____   _____   _____

And last but not least, once your student has completed his explanations, have him write a longer essay on the animals he likes the best after all of his research. This exercise should not only improve your student's vocabulary when it comes to animals, it should also get him interested in animals on a personal level, and this will help her remember what she has learned.

Word Whiz

Vocabulary Lists

This is not a dictionary! It is a list of 423 words important for grade school students to know. All of the words in the book's exercises are listed back here, along with other words your student should know when:

- **doing homework assignments**
- **taking tests at school**
- **preparing for and taking the STAR Program test**

All of these words should become part of your student's vocabulary.

I have written one or two "everyday" definitions for each word, along with sample sentences and illustrations here and there for the toughest ones.

If your kid—or you!—needs the pronunciation help or a more complete definition for a word, use a dictionary.

Word Whiz List
Test Instructions

another *n.*—an additional one. *Example:* Find <u>another</u> example of imperialism in the following passage.

belong *v.*—to be a part of. *Example:* Which of the following sentences does NOT <u>belong</u>.

bottom *n.*—the lowermost position. Opposite of *top*.

correct *adj.*—right. *Example:* Pick the <u>correct</u> answer from the following answer choices.

error *n.*—mistake. *Example:* Find the <u>error</u> in the writer's analysis.

fact *n.*—something that actually happened or exists. *Example:* Which of the following statements is a <u>fact</u>, according to the passage:

false *adj.*—not true. *Example*: From the passage you just read, which of these statements is <u>false</u>?

incorrect *adj.*—wrong. *Example:* Which of the answers are correct and which are <u>incorrect</u>?

information *n.*—the assembled knowledge provided in a test question. *Example:* According to the <u>information</u> in the passage, why do cats have claws? ,

inside *adv.*—on the interior. *Example:* Write your answer <u>inside</u> the square.

instructions *n.*—directions. *Example:* Make sure you read the <u>instructions</u> before answering the following questions.

main idea *n.*—the major, important idea. *Example*: What is the <u>main idea</u> of Part One?

main reason *n.*—the number one reason. *Example:* What is the author's <u>main reason</u> for writing his essay?

mainly *adv.*—for the most part. *Example:* Given the president's opinions about China, which of the following sentences is <u>mainly</u> correct?

middle *adj.*—the center. *Example:* Which line passes through the <u>middle</u> of the circle?

most *adv.*—greatest in number or size. *Example:* If Todd and Farrah each eat one-third of their pickles, who will have the <u>most</u> pickles left over?

most likely *adv.*—probably. *Example:* Which number would Julie most likely see on the next door?

mostly *adv.*—mainly; for the most part. *Example:* What is this story mostly about?

necessary *adj.*—required; needed. *Example:* Provide the numbers that are necessary to complete the pattern.

next *adj.*—following in order. *Example:* Pick the next number in the number sequence below.

opinion *n.*—what a person thinks, regardless of the facts. *Example*: It is my opinion that the Raiders have the best team in the NFL this year, even if their record doesn't show it.

outside *adv.*—on the exterior. *Example:* How many marbles are outside of the shape?

probably *adv.*—most likely. *Example:* What will Kevin probably do next?

same *adj.*—alike. *Example:* How are a dog and a cat the same?

top *n.*—the uppermost position. The opposite of *bottom*.

true *adj.*—correct. *Example:* Which statement is true about the first Spaniards who arrived in South America?

value *n.*—an assigned numerical quantity. *Example:* If $d = 4$, what is the value of $3.5 + d$?

Word Whiz List
English-Language Arts

abbreviation *n.*—a shorter way of writing a word. *Example: Mr.* is an abbreviation of *Mister*.

adjective *n.*—a word that describes a noun or a pronoun. *Example*: That's a *dirty* dog.

adverb *n.*—a word that modifies a verb, adjective, or another adverb. *Example:* That's a *really* dirty dog.

alliteration *n.*—the use of a series of words with the same first letter. *Example:* Simply said, Simon was seriously sick.

antonym *n.*—the opposite of a word. *Example: mean/nice.*

author *n.*—someone who writes books, plays, speeches, or articles.

autobiography *n.*—a biography written by the person it's about.

biography *n.*—a story of someone's life.

body (of a letter) *n.*—the middle section of a letter, which contains the main points of the letter.

capitalize *v.*—to make a letter uppercase.

chapter *n.*—a main section of a book.

character *n.*—a person in a book, play, movie, or TV show.

chronological *adj.*—arranged in order of when things occurred.

closure (of a letter) *n.*—the final section of a letter, which brings it to an end.

compare *v.*—to consider the similarities between things. On tests, compare is often used with *contrast. Example:* Compare and *contrast* the views of Writer A and Writer B.

conjunction *n.*—a word joining other words together in a sentence. *Example:* Bob and Shanyce wanted cookies, but their mom gave them carrots instead.

conscience *n.*—something inside you that knows the difference between right and wrong.

consistent *adj.*—staying the same.

consonant *n.*—a letter of the alphabet that isn't a vowel.

contrast *v.*—to look at the differences between things. On tests, contrast is often used with *compare. Example: Compare* and contrast the views of Writer A and Writer B.

description *n.*—explanation. *Example:* From the <u>description</u> above, how does an airplane land?

detail *n.*—a small part of a bigger whole. On tests, students are often asked to find <u>details</u> in a piece of writing that support the students' answers.

dialogue *n.*—the speaking parts in a book, play, movie, or TV show.

draft *n.*—the first version of a piece of writing. *Example*: Jill wrote a <u>draft</u> of her essay, then went back and wrote a final version

drama *n.*—a written performance for the theater, television, or cinema.

edit *v.*—to revise and correct a piece of writing.

evidence *n.*—the proof that something happened.

exclamation *n.*—something said strongly and loudly. In writing, an exclamation is expressed with an exclamation point!

fable *n.*—a story that uses characters to teach a lesson. *Example*: Aesop's <u>fables</u>.

familiar *adj.*—1) common. 2) having a good understanding of.

fantasy *n.*—1) an imaginary story. 2) the opposite of reality.

fiction *n.*—1) a story someone creates using his or her imagination. *Example*: The *Harry Potter* books are works of <u>fiction</u>. 2) a lie or untruth. *Example:* Separating fact from <u>fiction</u>.

folklore *n.*—stories handed down from generation to generation.

glossary *n.*—a list of words, along with their definitions, at the back of a book.

greeting (of a letter) *n.*—the salutation. The "Dear (blank)" part of the letter.

hero, heroine *n.*—the man (hero) or woman (heroine) who saves the day in a story.

humorous *adj.*—funny.

illustrator *n.*—someone who draws the pictures that go along with a story.

imagery *n.*—the act of painting a picture (image) with words. *Example:* At the climbers' high altitude, the stars <u>glittered like diamonds</u>.

imaginary *adj.*—not real; "in your head."

incomplete sentence *n.*—a sentence that is missing some of its necessary parts of speech.

index *n.*—the alphabetical list of a book's contents found in the back of a book.

influence *n.*—1) the power to affect an outcome. 2) *v.* to affect an outcome.

interview *n.*—a conversation in which someone asks all the questions and the other person answers them.

legend *n.*—the explanation of the symbols on a map.

legible *adj.*—readable. *Note:* It's important that your student's writing is <u>legible</u> so the teacher can read her answers.

limerick *n.*—a funny poem where lines 1, 2, and 5 rhyme with each other and lines 3 and 4 rhyme with each other.

Example: There once was a plumber named Ray
            Who fixed seven toilets a day.
            He came home one night
            And found something not right.
            His dog had run off with his pay.

margin *n.*—the blank space on the left or right hand side of a printed page. *Example:* Use the page's <u>margins</u> to take your notes and do any work.

metaphor *n.*—one thing related to something else. *Example:* Kobe Bryant is a *scoring machine*.

modifier *n.*—a word that affects the meaning of another word. *Example*: Adjectives, adverbs, and articles are all <u>modifiers</u>.

moral *n.*—the lesson a story or fable gets across. *Example*: The <u>moral</u> of the story? Never turn your back on an angry bear.

motivation *n.*—the reason a character in a story does what he does.

mysterious *adj.*—without an easy answer; hard to explain.

myth *n.*—a story that tries to explain the world or the universe. It usually involves gods, heroes, and adventures.

narrator *n.*—the teller of a story.

nonfiction *n.*—a true story.

noun *n.*—a word that names a person, place, or thing.

onomatopoeia *n.*—the use of words to imitate their meaning. *Examples:* *Buzz* and *splat*.

opinion *n.*—what someone thinks about something.

opposite *n.*—something completely different than something else.

pace *n.*—speed; rate. *Example:* Work at a fast and steady <u>pace</u>, and you should finish in plenty of time.

paraphrase *v.*—to restate using other words.

personification *n.*—the act of giving non-human things human characteristics.

persuade *v.*—to convince.

playwright *n.*—a person who writes plays.

plot *n.*—the events of a story.

plural *n.*—the form of a word that means "more than one." *Example*: The <u>plural</u> of *gopher* is *gophers*.

poem *n.*—a composition in either rhyming or free verse (no rhymes).

popular *adj.*—well-liked by many people.

possessive *n.*—a form of a word that shows possession. *Examples*: baker, *baker's* / me, *mine*.

prefix *n.*—a few letters added to the beginning of a word that change its meaning. *Examples:* dis- (*dis*ingenuous), ir- (*ir*retrievable), and de- (*de*claw) are examples of prefixes.

preposition *n.*—a word that relates a noun or pronoun to another word. *Example*: Ronnie ran and got help *for* Keith when Keith got *in* trouble.

pronoun *n.*—a word that takes the place of a noun. *Examples*: milk = *it*; Harold = *he* .

proper noun *n.*—the name of a specific person, place, or thing.

punctuation *n.*—the parts of a sentence that aren't words. *Examples:* period, comma, question mark.

revise *v.*—to change in order to improve; to amend.

rhyme *v.*—to link words that sound alike. *Example*: I tried to hit the rat with my bat. Imagine that.

rhythm *n.*—1) a regular pattern. 2) in music, a pattern of beats.

run-on sentence *n.*—a sentence that goes on too long, usually by using too many conjunctions. *Example:* I was going to go to sleep and there was a thunder storm and I got scared so I couldn't sleep.

salutation *n.*—a letter's greeting; the "Dear (blank)" part of the letter.

scene *n.*—a small section of a movie, play, or TV show.

setting *n.*—the place a story takes place.

simile *n.*—an explanation that uses the words "like" or "as." *Example:* Her hair is *as soft as silk.*

singular *adj.*—related to one of something.

suffix *n.*—a few letters added to the end of a word to change its meaning. –ness (bitter*ness*), -ly (like*ly*), and –ion (tens*ion*) are examples of suffixes.

suggest *v.*—to offer for consideration.

summarize *v.*—to write a shorter version of a long piece of writing where you just cover the main points.

support *v.*—to give evidence proving or explaining something. *Example:* Please support your theory that girls are much better than boys.

syllable *n.*—one chunk of a word that makes up single sound. The syllables in syllable are *syl, la,* and *ble.*

synonym *n.*—a word that means about the same thing as another. *Examples*: *smart* and *intelligent*; *couch* and *sofa*; *road* and *street.*

table of contents *n.*—the listing of chapters in the beginning of a book.

title *n.*—the name of a book or story.

verb *n.*—an action word. *Examples*: run, spell, consider.

vowel *n.*—the letters that aren't consonants, namely a, e, i, o, and u (and sometimes y).

Word Whiz List

Math

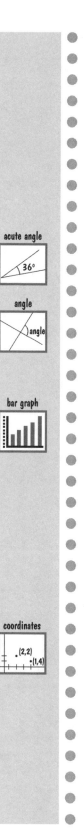

acute angle *n.*—an angle less than 90°.

addition *n.*—the act of combining two or more numbers. *Example*: 11 + 13 = 24.

angle *n.*—the figure made where two straight lines meet.

area *n.*—the amount of space inside a triangle, rectangle, circle, etc.

average *n.*—the number you get by adding two or more numbers, then dividing by how many numbers you added up. *Example*: The average of the numbers 4, 6, 8 and 10 is 7. (4 + 6 + 8 + 10 = 28. 28 ÷ 4 = 7.)

balance *n.*—what is left over; the remainder.

bar graph *n.*—a graph that looks like steps, with one quantity measured on the *x*-axis and the other on the *y*-axis.

circle *n.*—a perfectly round shape.

circle graph *n.*—a graph that shows proportions by dividing a circle into "slices." Otherwise known as a pie chart.

circumference *n.*—the length of the boundary of a circle.

combine *v.*—to add together.

cone *n.*—an object with a round base at one end and a point at the other. *Example*: An ice cream cone.

congruent *adj.*—usually used with triangles, means having the same shape. *Example*: If you lay one congruent triangle on top of another, they match exactly.

coordinates *n.*—the points on a graph.

cube *n.*—an object with six square faces, all the same size. *Example*: A sugar cube.

cylinder *n.*—an object shaped like a tube, with a circle at each end. *Example*: A toilet paper roll is a cylinder.

data *n.*—the facts and figures in a math problem.

decimal *n.*—1) a different way to write a fraction. 2) the part after the period in a number. *Examples*: .20, 3.45, –10.5

denominator *n.*—the number on the bottom of a fraction; the divisor.

diagonal *n.*—the line slanting from one corner to another corner of a four-sided figure.

diameter *n.*—the distance across the center of a circle.

digit *n.*—1, 2, 3, 4, 5, 6, 7, 8, 9, and 0 are digits.

dimensions *n.*—the length, width, and height of something.

dividend *n.*—a number to be divided by another; the number on the top in a fraction.

division *n.*— the act of "cutting" one number with another. *Example*: $4 \div 2 = 2$.

divisor *n.*—the number that is divided into the dividend.

double *v.*—to multiply by two.

dozen *n.*—the same as saying "12."

equal *adj.*—the same.

equation *n.*—1) a "math sentence." 2) a math statement where two quantities are equal to each other. *Example*: $2 \times 4 = 8$.

equilateral triangle

equilateral triangle *n.*—a triangle with all three sides the same length.

equivalent *adj.*—the same.

estimate *v.*—1) to guess; to come as close as possible to the real answer. 2) *n.* an educated guess.

even numbers *n.*—a number that can be divided evenly by two (no remainder). *Examples*: 2, 4, 6, 18, 20, 22.

exponent *n.*—the itty bitty little number attached to the upper right of a numeral that indicates the number of times to multiply a number by itself. *Example:* $12^4 = 12 \times 12 \times 12 \times 12$.

faces *n.*—the flat sides of a three-dimensional figure like a cube or a pyramid.

fraction *n.*—1) two numbers with a line between them. 2) part of a whole number. *Examples*: 1/2, 5/4, –1/6.

factor *n.*—1) a number that is multiplied by another number to get a product. *Example:* 1, 2, 7, and 14 are the factors for the number 14: (2 x 7 = 14) (1 x 14 = 14). 2) *v.* to break down a number into its factors.

hexagon

hexagon *n.*—a figure with six sides.

horizontal *adj.*—going left to right (or right to left!).

inequality *n.*—a math problem where one quantity is set as less than or greater than another quantity. *Example:* 8 > y. 2y < 22.

integer *n.*—a whole number (not a fraction or a decimal).

isosceles triangle

isosceles triangle *n.*—a triangle with two sides of equal length.

line graph *n.*—a graph where points are connected with a line. Usually looks like a mountain or hill, or slopes up or down.

linear *adj.*—of or like a line.

mass *n.*—the size and the bulk of something.

mean *n.*—the average of a group of numbers. (See the definition of *average* for an example.)

median *n.*—the middle one in a group of numbers, so the same number of numbers is above and below it.

mode *n.*—in a group of numbers, the one that occurs the most number of times.

multiplication *n.*—the addition of numbers together a bunch of times. *Example*: 3 x 5 means adding 3 to itself 5 times (3 + 3 + 3 + 3 + 3).

negative number *n.*—1) a number less than zero. 2) a number with a minus sign in front of it. *Examples*: –4, –23.3, –400, –.4, –3/4

number sentence *n.*—a mathematical operation. *Example:* 8 + 4 = 12.

numeral *n.*—a symbol used for a quantity. *Examples:* 1, 2, and 3 are numerals. X, V, and I are Roman numerals.

numerator *n.*—the number on top in a fraction; the dividend.

obtuse angle *n.*—an angle bigger than 90°.

octagon *n.*—an eight-sided shape.

odd number *n.*—a number that, when divided by 2, gives you a remainder. *Examples*: 1, 3, 5 . . . 19, 21, 23.

opposite *adj.*—directly across from.

ordered pair *n.*—the (*x,y*) on a number plane. (See the definition for *coordinates*.)

ordinal number *n.*—a number that shows position in a series. *Example*: The third hitter in an inning. The eighth planet in the solar system.

organize *v.*—to arrange in order.

pair *n.*—two of something. *Example*: A pair of shoes.

parallel *adj.*—relating to two lines in the same plane that never meet. *Example:* Train tracks are parallel to each other.

parallelogram *n.*—a four-sided shape, with the top and bottom parallel, and the sides parallel. *Note:* Often looks like a "tilted rectangle."

pattern *n.*—something repeating itself.

pentagon *n.*—a five-sided shape.

percent *n.*—1) per 100. 2) the expression of a fraction as a decimal.

perimeter *n.*—the boundary of a shape.

perpendicular *adj.*—intersecting at a 90° angle.

pie chart, pie graph *n.*—a circular chart where the pieces stand for percentages. *Note:* Looks like a pizza.

place value *n.*—the place a numeral sits in a number. *Example:* The place value of 4 in 4,123 is *thousands*. The place value of 3 in 673 is *ones*.

plane *n.*—a flat surface. *Note:* Think of the Great *Plains*.

polygon *n.*—a shape with three or more sides.

positive number *n.*—1) a number greater than zero. 2) any number WITHOUT a minus sign.

predict *v.*—to figure out how something will happen. *Example:* If Joe eats four pizzas a day, predict how many he will eat in three days.

prime factor *n.*—one of the smallest factors that make up a number.

obtuse angle

octagon

parallelogram

pentagon

perpendicular

Example: The prime factors of 64 are 2 x 2 x 2 x 2 x 2 x 2. So 2 is a prime factor of 64.

prism *n.*—a transparent solid object that breaks light up into a band of colors.

probability *n.*—odds. *Example:* Given their track record, what is the probability that Jane will beat Jack in the 50-meter dash?

pyramid *n.*—an object with triangles for its sides and a polygon for its base. *Note:* Think of the Great Pyramids of Egypt.

quadrilateral *n.*—a shape with four sides.

quotient *n.*—the answer to a division problem.

radius *n.*—the distance from the center to the edge of a circle.

random *adj.*—in no particular order.

ratio *n.*—the relationship between two quantities. *Example:* 15 students per one teacher = 15:1 student/teacher ratio.

rectangle *n.*—a shape with four sides and four right angles. *Note:* Each set of parallel sides has the same length.

remainder *n.*—the number left over in a division problem.

represent *v.*—to take the place of. *Example:* In this problem, *q* represents the number 4.

result *n.*—answer.

rhombus *n.*—a shape with all four sides the same length. *Note:* Often looks like a "tilted square" or a diamond.

right angle *n.*—a 90° angle. A right angle is formed when two lines intersect perpendicularly.

rotate *v.*—to turn on an axis. *Note:* On the STAR, figures are sometimes rotated.

round *adj.*—1) having no corners, like a circle. 2) *v.* to estimate by going up or down to the closest number. *Example:* If you are rounding to the nearest whole number, 6.75 rounds up to 7. If you are rounding down to the nearest tens place, 112 rounds down to 110.

scale *n.*—correct proportion. *Example:* I have a model of a Japanese Zero plane that is 1/8 the scale of a real one.

scalene triangle *n.*—a triangle with three unequal sides and three unequal angles.

segment *n.*—part of a line, usually marked with points.

similar *adj.*—sharing traits. *Note:* Usually used with *similar triangles*, whose sides have the same proportions.

sphere *n.*—a 3-D circle. *Note:* Think of a basketball or baseball.

square root *n.*—the number you multiply by itself to get a given value. *Example:* $\sqrt{4} = 2$ (because 2 x 2 = 4).

subtraction *n.*—the act of taking one number away from another. *Example:* 12 − 3 = 9.

sum *n.*—the result of addition. The sum of 4 + 5 is 9.

quadrilaterals

radius

rhombus

segment

symbol *n.*—something that stands for something else.

symmetry *n.*—sameness on each side of a dividing line.

three-dimensional *adj.*—having volume and depth. *Example*: A sphere is three-dimensional.

trapezoid *n.*—a quadrilateral with two parallel sides.

trapezoid

triangle *n.*—a three-sided figure.

two-dimensional *adj.*—on a single plane; having no volume. *Example*: A circle is two-dimensional.

variable *n.*—something with a value that can vary (change). In math, variables are usually called x and y.

vertical *adj.*—pointing straight up and down.

volume *n.*—the amount of space a 3-D object occupies.

whole number *n.*—an integer; a number that is not a fraction or a decimal.

Word Whiz List

History-Social Science

A.D. *adv.*—stands for "Anno Dominus." Also written sometimes as CE ("Common Era"). You count forward in "A.D. time," so A.D. 50 happened *before* A.D. 100. *Note:* A.D. precedes the year it identifies, but B.C. follows the year (see below).

adapt *v.*—to change to meet a new challenge or change in circumstance.

agriculture *n.*—the act of growing crops and raising livestock. *Example:* An agrarian society revolves around agriculture.

alliance *n.*—the joining of nations or people to achieve a goal. *Example:* On the TV show *Survivor*, contestants have to form alliances to protect themselves from the others.

amendment *n.*—a change that corrects or improves something. *Note*: Most often used on tests to describe an amendment to the Constitution.

ammunition *n.*—anything that can be shot from a gun or a cannon.

architecture *n.*—a style of building.

assemble *v.*—to gather together.

barter *v.*—to pay for stuff with other stuff, instead of with money. *Example*: Fred bartered for the Persian rug. He ended up paying the merchant two chickens and a goat for it.

boundary *n.*—the imaginary line that divides one country, state, or city from another.

boycott *v.*—to refuse to buy something or do something in protest.

budget *n.*—the plan for how a country—or person—will spend its money.

capitalism *n.*—an economic system that highlights private property—meaning people can own land and things.

century *n.*—a period of 100 years. *Note:* The century is "one more" than the number. 1671 is part of the 17th century. The year 1945 is part of the 20th century.

citizen *n.*—a member of a country or community. *Note:* Being a citizen usually brings with it defined rights and responsibilities.

civil rights *n.*—rights due a person because he is a citizen of a country. *Note*: It usually has to do with minorities' struggles for civil rights.

civilization *n.*—a group of people who have shown ability in language, agriculture, art, and commerce.

colonize *v.*—to start up a civilization somewhere new. *Note:* Usually refers to Europeans <u>colonizing</u> much of the globe in the 16th–19th centuries.

commerce *n.*—the buying and selling of goods and services.

communication *n.*—the act of exchanging information.

Congress *proper noun*—the U.S. Senate and House of Representatives. *Note*: <u>Congress</u> is one of the three branches of the U.S. government.

consequences *n.*—the results from an action.

conserve *v.*—to save by using sparingly.

Constitution *proper noun*—the rules around which the United States is built.

consumer *n.*—a person who buys goods and services.

continent *n.*—one of the seven major land masses on Earth: Africa, Antarctica, Asia, Australia, Europe, N. America, S. America.

cooperate *v.*—to work together.

credit *n.*—a system that allows you to buy something now and pay for it later.

customs *n.*—the traditions and behaviors of a country's citizens.

dam *n.*—a blockage in a stream or river.

debt *n.*—the money owed others.

decade *n.*—a period of ten years.

defense *n.*—the measures taken to protect something.

delegate *n.*—a representative; someone chosen to speak for others. *Example*: Elected officials are the <u>delegates</u> of the people.

democracy *n.*—a system of government based on the principle of equality where people hold the power.

desert *n.*—1) a dry, hot, sandy area. 2) *v.* to leave.

dictator *n.*—a single ruler of a country, usually mean and cruel.

discover *v.*—to find for the first time.

discrimination *n.*—the treatment of some people worse than others without a good reason. (See the definition for *prejudice*.)

domestic *adj.*—having to do with one's home or one's country. *Example:* Presidents have to deal with problems both foreign and <u>domestic</u>.

election *n.*—the casting of votes to choose among candidates.

eliminate *v.*—to get rid of.

empire *n.*—a group of countries and/or territories controlled by one country or ruler.

equator *n.*—an imaginary circle going around the middle of the Earth, the same distance from the North and South poles.

executive branch *n.*—the president and his staff. It is one of the three branches of federal government in the United States.

explorer *n.*—someone who searches out new places.

export *v.*—1) to sell something to someone outside your country. 2) *n.* something sold to another country.

federal *adj.*—having to do with a government that unites separate states under one central authority.

fertile *adj.*—able to produce crops (land) or offspring (organisms).

financial *adj.*—having to do with money and its management.

free enterprise *n.*—an economic system where people are free to buy and sell stuff for whatever price the other people are willing to pay.

freedom *n.*—the ability to say and do what you want.

goods *n.*—stuff that is bought and sold. In social studies, it is used in the phrase "goods and services" to describe the products of an economy.

government *n.*—the political system by which a city, state, or country is ruled.

hemisphere *n.*—one of the the two "halves" of the world divided by the equator. *Note:* The northern hemisphere contains the North Pole, and the southern hemisphere contains the South Pole.

heritage *n.*—traditions and customs handed down from generation to generation.

hostile *adj.*—relating to an enemy; unfriendly.

immigrate *v.*—to move to a foreign country.

immortal *adj.*—able to live forever.

imperialism *n.*—rule by a monarch (king or queen).

import *v.*—1) to bring something from one country to another. 2) *n.* something brought from one country into another.

independence *n.*—freedom.

industrial *adj.*—characterized by heavy industry, like car and steel manufacturing.

inhabitants *n.*—those who live somewhere.

integration *n.*—the joining of previously segregated black and white Americans in the 1960s.

invent *v.*—to create.

judicial branch *n.*—the system of courts in the U.S. *Note:* The judicial branch is one of the three branches of government.

latitude *n.*—the distance north or south of the equator, measured in degrees.

legend *n.*—the explanation of the symbols on a map.

legislature *n.*—a group of people (legislators) who make and change laws.

liberty *n.*—freedom.

longitude *n.*—the distance east and west of the prime meridian, measured in degrees.

majority *n.*—the biggest group of people. *Note*: In the U.S., the majority rules, but the minority also has rights.

medieval *adj.*—relating to the Middle Ages.

migration *n.*—the movement of a large group of people from one land to another.

militia *n.*—trained soldiers ready to fight at a moment's notice; an "on call" army.

minority *n.*—the smaller group of people.

mission *n.*—a place where missionaries live and work.

modify *v.*—to change; to alter.

monarchy *n.*—rule by a king or queen.

motto *n.*—a slogan or saying, usually used for self-identification. *Example:* Texas' state <u>motto</u> is "Don't mess with Texas."

nation *n.*—a country; people who live on the same land and have the same government.

navigate *v.*—to direct something (usually a ship) from one point to another.

negotiate *v.*—to work together to reach an agreement.

oppress *v.*—to prevent people from doing what they want to do.

patriotism *n.*—love of one's country.

persecute *v.*—to treat people very badly, usually because of their race or religion.

petition *n.*—a written request to a ruler or government.

pioneer *n.*—the first person to settle in a new land.

prejudice *n.*—thinking, for no good reason, that one group of people is better than another.

presidio *n.*—a fortress.

producer *n.*—in economics, the person or group of people that make the goods and provide the services. *Note*: In economics, <u>producer</u> is the "opposite" of consumer.

profit *n.*—the money one makes from selling something. *Example*: It cost Bette $3.00 to make that cake. She sold it for $7.00. That's a $4.00 <u>profit</u>!

prohibit *v.*—to not allow, to forbid.

propaganda *n.*—information that is supposed to make someone believe something; often an exaggeration of fact or just "one side of the story."

protect *v.*—to keep safe.

protest *v.*—1) to object strongly. 2) *n.* demonstration in the streets against something.

pueblo *n.*—a community of adobe and stone buildings built by the native peoples of America's Southwest.

rancho *n.*—a group of huts where ranch workers live.

ratify *v.*—to approve something and make it official.

reformer *n.*—someone who works to improve laws or customs.

Representatives, House of *proper noun*—one of two parts of the U.S. Congress. *Note*: In the House, states are proportionally represented: the bigger the state, the more representatives.

republic *n.*—a government made up of representatives elected by the people.

reservation *n.*—land a government reserves for a certain purpose. *Example:* Many Native Americans now live on <u>reservations</u>.

revolution *n.*—the overthrow of one government by a new one.

rural *adj.*—pertaining to the country (not the city).

scarce *adv.*—in short supply; not enough of something to go around to everyone who wants it.

segregation *n.*—the separation of one group of people from another. (See the definition for *integration*.)

self-evident *adj.*—obviously true.

Senate *proper noun*—one of two parts of the U.S. Congress. *Note*: Each state is represented by two senators in the <u>Senate</u>, regardless of its size.

services *n.*—labor. In social studies, it is used in the phrase "goods and <u>services</u>" to describe the products of an economy.

slavery *n.*—the ownership of one person or group of people by another.

strike *n.*—when workers all stop working at once. *Example:* Usually, people go on <u>strike</u> for better wages and better working conditions.

supply and demand *n.*—a law of economics used in a market economy. *Note:* When demand for a product goes up, its supply must also increase, or the product will get more expensive.

surrender *v.*—to give up.

tax *n.*—money paid by people that goes to fund their government.

technology *n.*—things learned through science that get applied in the real world.

timeline *n.*—a special graph that shows events along a line, in the order they occurred.

tolerant *adj.*—allowing people to live by codes and customs that are different from your own.

trade *n.*—the buying and selling of goods and services. *v.*—to give something and get something in return.

tradition *n.*—a way of doing things, passed down from generation to generation. (See the definition for *customs*.)

traitor *n.*—a person who betrays a country or a cause. *Example*: The most famous <u>traitor</u> of the Revolutionary War is Benedict Arnold.

transcontinental *adj.*—across a continent.

transportation *n.*—anything that moves something from here to there. *Examples*: Planes, trains, and cars are forms of <u>transportation</u>.

treason *n.*—the crime of being a traitor.

truce *n.*—a temporary fighting stoppage. *Note*: Wars usually have a bunch of <u>truces</u> before somebody finally surrenders for good.

tyranny *n.*—a government in which one person rules over everyone, and that one person is not very nice.

unalienable rights *n.*—rights that can never be taken back or ignored.

union *n.*—a group of individuals who band together to protect their interests.

volunteer *n.*—1) someone who does something just because she wants to help, usually without pay. 2) *v.* to join a cause of your own volition.

Word Whiz List

Science

amphibian *n.*—a cold-blooded animal that breathes with gills when it's young, and with lungs when it's older.

astronomy *n.*—the study of the universe.

atom *n.*—the smallest unit of an element.

attract *v.*—to draw closer. In science, magnets are used to <u>attract</u> metals. The opposite of <u>attract</u> is *repel*.

buoyancy *n.*—the ability of something to float.

carnivore *n.*—an animal that eats meat.

circuit *n.*—a closed path that electricity flows through.

conduct *v.*—to help something go from one place to another.

conservation *n.*—the protection and preservation of natural resources.

decompose *v.*—to break down. In science, it usually refers to dead animals and plants <u>decomposing</u>.

dissolve *v.*—to disintegrate into tiny particles and mix into a liquid. (See *soluble*.)

diversity *n.*—variety. *Example*: The Earth supports a <u>diversity</u> of living organisms.

eclipse *n.*—the blockage of light from the sun. *Example*: A solar <u>eclipse</u> is caused by the moon passing between the Earth and the sun.

ecosystem *n.*—a group of plants, animals, and environmental factors that affect one another.

electromagnet *n.*—a magnet that uses electricity to create its magnetic force.

energy *n.*—1) usable heat. 2) electricity.

environment *n.*—a person's, animal's, or plant's surroundings.

erosion *n.*—the process of wearing something away a little at a time.

evaporation *n.*—the process of liquid changing to gas.

experiment *n.*—a test performed to prove something.

external *adj.*—having to do with the outside of something. *Example:* The otter's habitat is affected by <u>external</u> forces, including pollution from a nearby power plant and noise from a nearby highway.

fish *n.*—a large group of cold-blooded animals with gills and fins that live and reproduce in the water.

food chain *n.*—a series of animals and plants that eat each other; the cycle of life.

fungi *n.*—the plural of fungus. Fungus is not a plant or an animal. It is a third kind of organism. *Example:* The most common examples of fungi are mushrooms and mold.

gas *n.*—a substance can be either a solid, a liquid, or a gas. Gas is the least dense of the three forms. A gas can expand to fill a container. It is typically invisible and sometimes has an odor.

grassland *n.*—a large area covered with grass.

herbivore *n.*—an animal that eats plants.

identical *adj.*—the same.

igneous rock *n.*—rock that is made of hardened liquified rock (magma). *Example:* Basalt is an igneous rock.

increase *v.*—to make bigger.

insect *n.*—a group of small hard-shelled animals with three pairs of legs, a segmented body, and, usually, a pair of wings.

internal *adj.*—having to do with the inside of something. *Example:* The otter developed internal injuries from living in the polluted environment. Its stomach's lining was burned through from drinking so much dirty water.

learned *adj.*—acquired through experience. *Example:* The traits you are not born with are learned, such as your ability to read.

liquid *n.*—a substance can be either a solid, a liquid, or a gas. Liquid flows, like water (which is, of course, a liquid), is denser than gas, but less dense than a solid.

lunar *adj.*—having to do with the moon.

magnetic *adj.*—having the ability to attract other things.

magnify *v.*—to make something look bigger. *Example:* My magnifying glass magnified the wolf spider to ten times its size. That's when I dropped the magnifying glass and started screaming. That was embarrassing.

mammal *n.*—a warm-blooded animal, usually with hair, that gives birth to live offspring.

matter *n.*—something that has weight and volume.

metamorphic rock *n.*—igneous rock that is changed into another kind of rock because of extreme pressure. *Example:* Marble is a metamorphic rock; it is smashed and heated limestone.

omnivore *n.*—an animal that eats both plants and other animals.

organism *n.*—a living thing. *Examples:* Plants, animals, and fungi are all organisms.

pollinate *v.*—to fertilize a plant with pollen.

predator *n.*—an animal that hunts other animals for food.

prediction *n.*—an educated guess about something in the future.

prey *n.*—the animal or animals a predator hunts for food.

properties *n.*—attributes.

reclaim *v.*—to take back. *Example:* California is working to <u>reclaim</u> some marshland that was lost to development.

recycle *v.*—to use again.

reduce *v.*—to make smaller.

reliable *adj.*—trustworthy.

renewable *adj.*—able to be used again or to be replaced by new growth. *Example*: Trees are <u>renewable</u> resources because you can always grow new ones.

repel *v.*—to force away from. *Example:* While magnets attract some metals, they <u>repel</u> each other.

reptile *n.*—a cold-blooded animal that breathes with lungs and is usually covered with scales.

reservoir *n.*—a lake or pool that collects water.

sedimentary rock *n.*—rock formed from compressed sediments. *Example*: Sandstone and limestone are <u>sedimentary rocks</u>. Sandstone is made from sand; limestone is made from fragments of sea creatures.

shelter *n.*—a protective dwelling.

solar system *n.*—the sun, the group of planets, and the other heavenly bodies surrounding our sun. *Note: solar* means *sun*.

solid *n.*—a substance can be either a solid, a liquid or a gas. A solid has a definite shape and weight. It has the highest density of the three forms of matter.

soluble *n.*—able to be dissolved in something else. *Example:* Salt is <u>soluble</u> in water.

texture *n.*—the feel of a surface. Paper has a smooth <u>texture</u>. Sandpaper has a rough *texture*.

tundra *n.*—an arctic area with no trees and few plants.

wetlands *n.*—a marsh or swampy area saturated with water.

Notes/Words

Use these pages for the exercises or to write down words
your student is having trouble with that aren't in this book.

Notes/Words

Also Available